Loften Mitchell
Tell Pharaoh

BROADWAY PLAY PUBLISHING INC
224 E 62nd St, NY, NY 10065
www.broadwayplaypub.com
info@broadwayplaypub.com

TELL PHARAOH

© Copyright 1986 by Loften Mitchell

All rights reserved. This work is fully protected under the copyright laws of the United States of America.

No part of this publication may be photocopied, reproduced, stored in a retrieval system, or transmitted, in any form or by any means, electronic, mechanical, recording, or otherwise, without the prior permission of the publisher. Additional copies of this play are available from the publisher.

Written permission is required for live performance of any sort. This includes readings, cuttings, scenes, and excerpts. For amateur and stock performances, please contact Broadway Play Publishing, Inc. For all other rights contact: Walter Gidaly, 750 Third Avenue, New York, NY 10015.

First printing: April 1987
ISBN: 0-88145-048-0

Design by Marie Donovan
Set in Aster by L&F Technical Composition, Lakeland, FL
Printed on acid-free paper and bound by BookCrafters, Inc., Chelsea, MI

Dedication

To the memory of my parents,
Willia and Ulysses Mitchell

To my sister, Gladys, and her husband,
Herman Blair, and to my brothers,
Clayton, Louis, and Melvin

and

To the people of Harlem and their
many friends, living and dead,
and to generations yet unborn,

And to the brilliant and beautiful
Deanna Fix France

About the Author

Loften Mitchell is Professor Emeritus, Department of Theater, at the State University of New York at Binghamton. The author of numerous plays, musicals, and books, his musical *Bubbling Brown Sugar* (Broadway Play Publishing, 1984) was nominated for the 1976 Tony Award. The work was awarded Best Musical of the year 1977 in London.

Mitchell's other plays include *A Land Beyond the River* (1957; Pioneer Drama Service, Denver, CO); *The Phonograph* (1969), a family play; *The Final Solution to the Black Problem in the United States, or the Fall of the American Empire* (1970); *Sojourn to the South of the Wall* (1973), a play about Black people in seventeenth-century New Amsterdam; *The Cellar* (1952), which was produced at the Harlem Showcase Theatre; and *The Bancroft Dynasty* (1948), at the 115th Street Peoples' Theatre.

In addition to *Bubbling Brown Sugar*, Mr. Mitchell's musicals include the 1983 production, *Miss Ethel Waters*; *A Gypsy Girl* (1982), which was produced in Pine Bluff, Arkansas; *Cartoons for a Lunch Hour* (1978), at New York's Perry Street Theatre; *Star of the Morning* (1964), a musical play about Bert Williams, with music by Louis Mitchell and lyrics by Romare Bearden and Clyde Fox. Mr. Mitchell also collaborated with John Oliver Killens on *Ballad of the Winter Soldiers*, produced at Lincoln Center, starring Robert Ryan, Shelley Winters, Ruby Dee, Dick Gregory, Frederick O'Neal, and others. In conjunction with composer Irving Burgie, *Ballad for Bimshire* was produced on Broadway in 1963, with Ossie Davis, Frederick O'Neal, and Robert Hooks heading the cast.

Mr. Mitchell attended the New York City public schools, Talladega College, and Columbia University. He won the 1958–59 Guggenheim Award for Creative Writing in the Drama, and subsequent awards from the Rockefeller Foundation, the Harlem Cultural Council, the Audience Development Committee, and the State University of New York Research Award. His books include: *Black Drama, The Stubborn Old Lady Who Resisted Change,* and *Voices of the Black Theatre.*

Acknowledgments

During a nineteen-sixties interview with the great Yankee catcher, Elston Howard, on a night in his honor, I was told: "Just thank everybody for me. You can do it better than I can."

I tried, then, but I don't think I was very successful. I am certain that I am not going to be successful now. There are more sources for this work than I can possibly remember. Certainly H.L. Dixon's *History of New York*, J.A. Roger's pioneering studies, Claude McKay's *Harlem: Negro Metropolis*, James Weldon Johnson's *Black Manhattan*, John Henrik Clarke's *Harlem U.S.A.*, Gilbert Osofsky's *The Making of a Ghetto*, James E. Allen's *The Negro in New York*, Jervis Anderson's *This Was Harlem*, and the essays of Ted Poston and Henry Lee Moon have strongly influenced this writing. So, too, has the brilliant writing of the great Dr. William Edward Burghardt Du Bois.

So, too, have the Schomburg Collection, the Association for the Study of Negro Life and History, and the Emanuel Pieterson Historical Society. There also were numerous street club leaders of the earlier days—men like Andrew M. Burris, Glenn Carrington, Zell Ingram, and others—who brought writers Langston Hughes, Countee Cullen, and others to our meetings, lighting and re-lighting the torch of heritage and identity.

There were still others whose names fade away but whose comments live on and on. They sat around in churches and other institutions, sharing memories of an event here, one there. Their contributions were, indeed, greater than they knew, and even today

I stand, teary-eyed, when I see a lonely figure standing on a streetcorner, never knowing the contributions he has made to scores of others.

Binghamton, NY
April 1987

LOFTEN MITCHELL

Tell Pharaoh and Past Productions

"There will be no next time!"
This declaration was made by this writer backstage at the Queens College Colden Auditorium on February 19, 1967. A jam-packed audience had given the cast of *Tell Pharaoh* a standing ovation. Cast members crowded around the backstage area, talking about "the next time we do this show." I reminded them this was a benefit, a one-time affair. I was glad it was over.

It started innocuously. In early 1967 executives of the National Association for the Advancement of Colored People's Jamaica Chapter called me to a meeting. Present were civic leader Peter Saltz, attorney Wilson Eugene Sharpe, educator Robert Couche, and poets Dan Simmons and James C. Morris. They outlined a plan for five Long Island NAACP Chapters to sponsor a Negro-History Brotherhood Program at Queens College's Colden Auditorium. I was invited to serve as a consultant.

I accepted, willingly, knowing this meant no *real* work. The previous year had been overburdening. I completed the book, *Black Drama*, wrote for *Crisis Magazine* and the *New York Amsterdam News*, taught playwriting at Louis Gossett Jr.'s Academy of Dramatic Arts, and wrote the first version of *Ballad of a Blackbird*—which became *Bubbling Brown Sugar* eight years later. I was not interested in any kind of work. So—I recommended a group of actors these executives might consider for the program, then left the meeting, believing my "work" was done.

It was not. The following week Ruby Dee, Frederick O'Neal, Micki Grant, Louis Gossett, Jr., and Diana Sands called me, wanting to know what I was writing for them to read on February 19. I hemmed and hawed as I realized that an NAACP official had called these artists, invited them to appear, then mentioned that I was writing a special play for the occasion.

It was too late to turn back. I had to write *something*. I decided to take a few pages of *Black Drama*, write a narration, and have the actors read this. It did not take long for me to realize that this did not work. A series of conferences with the NAACP officials revealed that the organization was primarily interested in stories about the development of various Black neighborhoods. That led me back to a piece I had written for the New York Urban League in the early nineteen-sixties, *Operation Open City*. This concert drama about the need for housing starred Micki Grant, Albert Grant, and Gertrude Parthenia McBrown and was presented at New York's Ethical Culture Society.

This material plus some from *Black Drama* and some from *Ballad of the Winter Soldiers* merged into what became *Tell Pharaoh*. This concert drama had sections to be read from lecterns, others to be acted out, all interspersed with Negro spirituals. On a cold, snowy day the following professionals appeared: Ruby Dee, Micki Grant, Louis Gossett, Jr., Frederick O'Neal, Gloria Daniel, Mary Alyce Glenn, singers Robert Alexander and Lucille Burney, and the St. Albans Children's Choir. My late brother, Melvin Mitchell, stage managed the production. A movie commitment prevented Diana Sands from appearing.

Dignitaries and common folks, old folks and young folks, jammed Colden Auditorium. Their standing ovation led to the cast talking about "the next time we do this" and to my reply:

"There will be no next time!"

I was wrong again. Two of my wife's relatives, Jo and Milton Coulthurst, joined Virginia and James Glass and presented *Tell Pharaoh* at the National Maritime Union Theatre on May 7, 1967. Albert Grant was director of this benefit for the Schomburg Collection.

That offering was exciting offstage as well as on. Ruby Dee, a New Rochelle resident, had no car that day. She asked for someone to pick her up and drive her to the theatre. It was a day of continuous, cold rain. I asked the producers to arrange transportation, but each had some very important dignitary who had to be given a ride to the theatre. Finally, I turned to my wife and laughed in spite of my annoyance. "My God!" I yelled. "The star of the show is up there in New Rochelle and can't get to the show, yet people are all running around picking up other people to come see her!"

"Let's be professional," said my wife. "Send a taxi for Ruby and bill the producers."

We did just that.

Again the show received a standing ovation from a packed house. Afterwards my brother, Melvin, introduced me to Mrs. Effie Hill Brown of Brooklyn's Concord Baptist Church. She invited us to perform there. And we did. And the offstage drama equaled the one on stage.

The sponsors were the Sisterhood of Concord Baptists Church. A group of cast members met and we patronized the hell out of the Sisters. We agreed to do the show for a flat six hundred dollars without a percentage. We declared we did not want to take advantage of the Sisters, but we *had* to have six hundred dollars if only *one* person showed up that night.

We learned a lesson. On a cold, rainy Autumn night production manager Billy Reed drove us to the theatre. We mourned for the Sisters. How could we take their money? Backstage we met with Ossie Davis, Hilda Simms, and McKinley Johnson who had joined our company. We agreed that "if push comes to shove, we'll forget our six hundred." Then, I went out into the audience to watch the first act.

There wasn't an empty seat in the house. People kept pouring into the place. The Sisters brought in folding chairs and more folding chairs. The Reverend Dr. Gardner Taylor, church pastor, said: "If one more person shows up, we'll have to put him on the ceiling."

That was only the beginning. During intermission the Sistes sold sandwiches and coffee. One stand collected forty dollars while I was standing there. At another stand people sold *Black Drama*—and had me autographing the book. Before the second act began the Sisters paid us six hundred dollars. We shook our heads in unison.

That, for me, was the end of *Tell Pharaoh*. Or, so I thought. Billy Reed went on a booking campaign and soon *Tell Pharaoh* was seen in a Bronx church, in Babylon, Long Island, and in Westchester County. And then came California. . . .

From June 17, 1968 to August 2, 1968 an Institute in Black Repertory Theatre was held on the campus of the University of California at Santa Barbara. This was spearheaded by Professor William R. Reardon of Santa Barbara, Professor Thomas D. Pawley of Lincoln University in Jefferson City, Missouri, and Professor Owen Dodson of Howard University. Produced that summer were my play, *A Land Beyond the River*, Ted Shine's *Morning, Noon and Night*, James V. Hatch and C. Bernard Jackson's musical, *Fly Blackbird*, and two concert readings: Ossie Davis' *Curtain Call, Mr. Aldridge, Sir*, and my *Tell Pharaoh*. This institute led to several productions of *Tell Pharaoh* because many participants took copies of the script home with them.

The Institute sent *Tell Pharaoh* into high gear. In 1969 H.D. Flowers directed and produced the work at South Carolina State College. Philadelphia impressario Samuel Evans had me adapt the script into *The Afro-Philadelphian* for production at the Academy of Music in 1970. Ruby Dee, Ossie Davis,

Hilda Simms, and Frederick O'Neal starred. In 1969 and 1970 Anthony O. Williams produced *Tell Pharaoh* in a San Francisco theatre, and then on NBC-TV. In 1971 there was a production at the State University of New York at Binghamton, starring Hilda Simms, Frederick O'Neal, Alice Childress, Julian Mayfield, and Beverly Penn. That summer Tommie Harris, formerly of the Santa Barbara Institute, produced the work at Jackson State College.

The summer of 1972 found *Tell Pharaoh* at the Yonkers Museum, sponsored by the Church of Our Saviour and the Reverend Nathaniel T. Grady. Billy Reed directed a cast that starred Frederick O'Neal, Hilda Simms, Mubarak Antar Mahmoud, Michelle Stent, Albert Grant, Bertha Jarvis, and pianist Earl Gordon. 1973 there was another Binghamton showing. In 1974 Gladys Blair presented Percival Borde's production at the Cathedral of St. John the Divine, starring gospel singer Gladys Brooks. In 1976 Curtis King, Jr. offered several showings in the Dallas, Texas area—productions that served to raise funds for the Junior Black Academy of Arts and Letters.

In 1978 Gladys Blair presented another Queens showing. 1980 brought a Talladega College production. 1981 saw theatre veteran Carl Lee direct the work for the Playwrights Program at the State University of New York at Binghamton. In 1982 *Tell Pharaoh* was part of a street theatre program in Jacksonville, Florida.

On June 21, 1984 Dick Gaffield and the American Folk Theatre presented Nora Cole, Frances Foster, Earle Hyman, and Jewdyer Osborne in *Tell Pharaoh* at New York City's Symphony Space. Oscar Brown, Jr. appeared in this and wrote a special number, *The Blues*, with lyrics by Deanna Fix France. Henry Miller directed and Horace Beasley was musical director. Marc Malamud created the sets and lighting effects and choir members Carl Murray, Joe

Ireland, and Lonni Clark of Canaan Baptist Church sang the spirituals.

An Oberlin College production, directed by Woodie King, Jr. followed. In April 1986 Gladys Blair and Jewdyer Osborne presented Micki Grant, Nora Cole, and Graham Brown in a New York production directed by LaTanya Richardson. This engagement was largely supported by Dick Campbell of the Sickle Cell Anemia Foundation of Greater New York and Horace Carter and the Emanuel Pieterson Historical Society. And this brought on requests for future productions. . . . and all these productions contributed to the rewriting of the play in August 1986, and the present publication.

All this is noted here by the author who said in 1967: "There will be no next time!"

Production Notes

The following notes have been reprinted from *The Black Teacher and the Dramatic Arts* (pp. 128–130), edited by William R. Reardon and Thomas D. Pawley, published by Greenwood Press in 1970.*

Tell Pharaoh may be performed in intimate surroundings but is also capable of being expanded for production in huge auditoriums. The key to this expansion lies in the producer's decision as to how the music should be handled. Large choral groups are definitely a potential for this show (the St. Albans Children's Choir was used in the original production), and music may be rendered by guitar accompaniment or *a cappella*. It is so tightly written that if the producer desires, and if the young woman and the young man are also singers, the entire show can be done with four people. However, even a quick reading will indicate the possibility for added magnitude present in the musical aspects of the show, and probably either choral groups or sound tapes of choral groups will be utilized most often. The staging itself is reasonably minimal, relying mainly upon the lecterns with an open area for the occasional scene that is played thereon. Some further potentials for effectiveness exist in the use of lighting designs for the areas.

Mitchell loves Harlem. No one who reads any of his works on Harlem can doubt that. But *Tell Pharaoh* is more than a loving depiction of Harlem— it is an impassioned cry for liberation, for justice. It shows a Harlem that is the hub of the black America

---

*Reprinted with permission by William R. Reardon and Thomas D. Pawley.

to which stream the exploited looking for a life with some hope for themselves and their children. It shows, too, how from its very start, Harlem has been sold out and its people "'buked and scorned" by those who sought only avaricious gain from the locale and inhabitants. History is called forth to attest to those who sold out the Negroes—the British, particularly, who, having seized New Amsterdam, brought into existence very severe slave codes. Even after glorious participation in the Revolution, harassments continued with the attacks of hoodlums on the African Grove Theatre and the African Free School. Even later, the contributions of the Negro to the battles in the Civil War were conveniently ignored.

To many people, the idea of Harlem as a suburban carriage and mansion area in the late nineteenth century will seem quite unusual. The exploitation of Harlem by real estate interests who knew how desperately the Negro needed an area for homes is not only stated but movingly depicted in scenes of a mother desirous of her daughter not being beat up on her way home from school, or of a father who, returning home angry, is told by his wife to "Go fight where you got mad!" and answers only, "If I did, you'd be a widow before you could bat an eye!" The Negro needed Harlem—and he paid for it at triple the normal price.

Still there was happiness—when the battling was over. And there were moments of great nostalgia as the beautiful people strolled on their Sunday walks, or indulged in their private language. But the harmony was disrupted beneath the blast of economic enslavement that came from foreclosures and refusals to grant loans on mortgages. As Mitchell puts it, "the rape of the black American was complete." But still the black community survived, and still, as World War II ends the first act, its young men go forth to fight for a democracy which is not theirs at home.

In his second act, Mitchell concerns himself with a problem of a more national scale—the decisions stemming from DeLaine's battle in South Carolina. The seeds of rebellion burst forth throughout the land, and although met by increased indignities and attempts at suppression, they will not be prevented from flowering. In the midst of his passion, Mitchell interjects the leavening humor of Black Sam the Cowboy and rises from that moment to a paean commanding Pharaoh to let my people go—all my peoples, everywhere, throughout the earth. *Tell Pharaoh* can be an intensely moving experience and affords an excellent opportunity for drama and musical groups to collaborate on production.

Tell Pharaoh
A Concert Drama

Characters

MISS BLACK—A woman in her twenties or thirties; a singer
MRS. BLACK—A woman in her forties
MR. BLACK SENIOR—A man in his forties or fifties
MR. BLACK JUNIOR—A man in his twenties or thirties; a singer-guitarist

Note: In the event Miss Black and Mr. Black, Junior are to be played by actors who do not sing, it is suggested that a female or male singer perform all the songs. The songs may be delivered with guitar accompaniment or rendered without accompaniment.

Various productions throughout the country have used full-scale choirs and dancers. On several occasions parts have been broken down, and as many as twelve actors were used in production.

In short, the play may be very simply produced or it may be elaborately done. This depends entirely upon the production concept.

Act One

(*There is no scenery. Four lecterns are onstage, two at stage left and two at stage right. There is a microphone in center stage.*)

(*Four actors take their places at the lecterns after the houselights dim. They are:* Miss Black, *a woman in her twenties or thirties;* Mrs. Black, *a woman in her forties;* Mr. Black, Junior *a man in his twenties or thirties; and* Mr. Black, Senior, *a man in his forties or fifties.*)

(*A strong, stirring note is heard on the guitar, playing the theme song of the play. Out of the darkness we hear* Miss Black *singing from center stage as the lights fade in.*)

Miss Black: (*Singing*)
When Israel was in Egypt land,
"Let my people go!"
Oppressed so hard they could not stand,
"Let my people go!"
"Go down, Moses,
'Way down in Egypt land,
Tell old pharaoh
To let my people go!"

(*The lights on her now dim as the music carries under. Lights come up on* Mrs. Black *as she stands at a lectern, stage right.*)

Mrs. Black: There is a beautiful hill at the northern end of Central Park. This hill is grass covered in the spring and summer, bare and brown in the autumn, and cold and foreboding in the winter. But—even in the winter when the earth is dark and cracked, you can look at that hill and know somehow that spring will come to it again and again the grass will be green. And as you look, you know that spring will come again and again.

MR. BLACK, SENIOR: (*At his lectern*) From that hilltop you can see all of Harlem. You look directly down on 110th Street and Seventh Avenue. Then—as your eyes gaze westward—you can see the Cathedral of St. John the Divine, Columbia University, and Morningside Heights. You look straight up Seventh Avenue and on a clear day you can see 125th Street, 135th Street, and 145th Street and on to where the Avenue runs into the Harlem River. As your eyes gaze eastward they pick out the Triboro Bridge spanning the East River, connecting Manhattan, and Bronx, and Queens. As your eyes move downtown again, you see Fifth Avenue, then Lenox Avenue at 110th Street.

MR. BLACK, JUNIOR: (*At his lectern*) All of Harlem is before you. Harlem with its swank apartment buildings, its monuments, its slums, its numerous buildings, and its proud history. For Harlem is many things to many people. Each time I read something about Harlem, I am reminded of a story my father used to tell:

SENIOR: A cruel slavemaster died. Now at his funeral the preacher raved and he ranted. He cried and he moaned. He talked about what a gentle soul the slavemaster was, about how kind he was, about the way he loved all mankind. Well, an old Negro slave woman sat there in the back of the church and she listened and she listened. Finally, she got up and ambled on out of that church. Back at the slave quarters she saw the other slaves singing and rejoicing and celebrating old master's death. The slave woman told them:

MRS. BLACK: "You all better get them grins off'n your faces. You think old master's dead, but he just liable not to be. That sure wasn't *him* that man's in church preaching about!"

ACT ONE

MISS BLACK: (*At her lectern*) Harlem certainly isn't analogous to a slave master, but the lies told about the community are as bizarre as those the minister told about the old master. These lies are products of the same structure which idolizes the slave owner and decries the enslaved!

MRS. BLACK:
Harlem. A gentle land, fertile with dreams,
Yet writhing in mightmarish pain.

JUNIOR:
Harlem. The modern slaver's whip lashes your
 young,
Your teen-agers, middle-agers, and your very old,
Sentencing them to abject poverty in the midst of
 plenty,
To hopelessness in a world of euphoria,
To powerlessness in a power-mad world!

MISS BLACK:
Harlem. A defiant land, laughing at hostility,
Challenging it, demanding universal manhood rights,
Demanding freedom now!

MRS. BLACK:
This land has been called evil,
But no lynch mobs mar its history.
It has been called a jungle,
But the snakes of Mississippi are more venoumous!

SENIOR:
It has been called a swampland,
But the Bowery and Forty-second Street devour
 more humanity.
It has been called a No Man's Land for whites,
But what are Palm Beach and Westchester and
 Roslyn Heights
For Black people?

MISS BLACK:
Harlem has even been called middle-class, yet
It could never be as much in the middle,

Signifying non-alignment and decadence as
Park Avenue and Madison Avenue and Fifth Avenue.

MRS. BLACK: Beautiful, Black Harlem. A Black woman. An innocent child.

JUNIOR:
A garrulous youth crying out
For his identity!

SENIOR:
A nationalist leader exhorting his people:
"Buy Black."

MISS BLACK:
And young people,
Old people,
Seeking leadership, demanding answers
To questions raised long, long ago.

SENIOR:
Wise, Black Harlem. Patient.
Repositer of a Black nations's wisdom.
The very heart and pulse of that Nation.

JUNIOR: Much studied, rarely understood Harlem.

MRS. BLACK:
Amused. Bemused. Refused.
Talked about, written about,
Purveyed. Surveyed.
Yet the truth lies hidden,
Hidden behind stacks of lies.
What is the truth about you, Harlem?
The truth is that you are what you are because
White America has never been honest in
Its treatment of Black people!

MISS BLACK: That's the truth!

JUNIOR: The whole truth!

SENIOR: Nothing but the truth!

MRS. BLACK:
White America, get off Harlem's back!
Get off every Black man and woman's back!
Get off! Get off!
And if you don't,
We're going to push you off!

(*A stirring note is heard as the lights begin to dim. Led by* MISS BLACK, *the group sings.*)

ALL:
Ohh, Freedom! Ohh, Freedom!
Oh, Freedom over me!
And before I'll be a slave,
I'll be buried in my grave
And go home to my Lord and be free!

(*The lights are down completely. Now, a spotlight comes up on* MRS. BLACK *at lectern:*)

MRS. BLACK: The history of Harlem is rooted in the birth of this nation. Africa's children contributed to that birth.... While Europe was a land peopled by what we today call barbarians, Africa had advanced civilization that could build pyramids, a Sphinx, smelt iron, and record human history. Later, too, there appeared the Songhay Empire, early Ghana, and the world's oldest university at Timbuktu. Its learned scholars had advanced knowledge of mathematics, astronomy, and other sciences. One such man, Ahmed Baba, wrote forty-seven books on forty-seven different subjects. His personal library of 1,600 books was destroyed when the Moors invaded Timbuktu.

MISS BLACK:
Restless is the child of the African mother—
Community-minded, generous to a fault,
Believing that the land belongs to all,
And all to the land.
Restless, indeed, is the child of the African mother,
Seeking to share his wealth in the midst of impoverishment,
Seeking to share the sunlight of his experience with those away from the sun.

MRS. BLACK:
Restless, indeed, is the child of the African mother—
He was Solomon and Sheba, Moses and Pharaoh—
He was Hannibal of Carthage invading Rome,
And he overran Spain—
He walked with the Christ
And he fought the Caesars.
Restless, indeed is the child of the African mother,
And many a professor and many an artisan journeyed north
To Crete,
To Phoenicia,
Greece and Rome,
To Civilize barbaric Europe,
To bring it human knowledge.

MISS BLACK:
Middle-aged Europe: Impoverished land,
War-torn, tradeless,
Going nowhere for it had nowhere to go—
Then—
Marco Polo and his adventures
Set tongues to wagging with lurid tales
Of endless oriental wealth,
And it is said that Christopher Columbus heard
Of a land to the west from his contact with Africans.

MRS. BLACK:
The Africanesque features of ancient Latin works
Suggest that Africa touched America
Long, long before Europe.
A man of African origin named Pietro captained one
    of Columbus' ships.

MISS BLACK:
There was a Black man with Ponce De Leon when he
    reached Florida in 1512
And one with Balboa when he "discovered" the
    Pacific.
And a man named Estevanico led an expedition from
    Mexico City

ACT ONE

Into what is now Arizona and New Mexico.
Let the record be read and read well,
For we helped to discover—or discovered
San Francisco,
Los Angeles,
Chicago,
Wisconsin,
Denver,
Pike's Peak,
And we brought the dawn to sleeping America.

MISS BLACK:
Let the record be read and read well:
This New World that Columbus allegedly discovered—
This Eldorado of the West was a vast wilderness,
A harsh, hideous world.
Forty-four Pilgrim fathers died their first winter
   here—
Only six or seven remained sound persons.

MRS. BLACK:
Neither the first white men here nor the red men
Could fell the forests,
Plant the crops
Nor build the cities
For this New World.
Senseless wars had wasted European men,
And there was only one place to turn for labor:
That place was Africa!

(*Music under, then it rises:*)

ALL: (*Singing*)
I'm gonna tell God all my troubles when I get home—
I'm gonna tell God all my troubles when I get home—
I'm gonna fall down on my knees and pray
'Cause I'm gonna meet Him on that Judgment Day—
I'm gonna tell God all my troubles when I get home—

MRS. BLACK: (*As music carries under*) Turn to Africa the Europeans did and they wrote in blood that savage crime known as chattel slavery. They dumped chained Black Africans into slave ship holds, transplanted them from the dark beauty of their motherland, and denied them their family ties, traditions, and cultural continuity. Black people were sold into southern and northern areas of the New World.

MISS BLACK:
I was in my own land and the white man came for me—
I was home under the moon and stars, completely free!

I danced there on a thousand moonlit nights
My Black soul sailed on a thousand flights—

The sun seemed to glow for just my people and me—
I was warmed by that sun in the land of the free.

The need for free labor made me into a slave—
The world forgot all—all that to it I gave.

They dumped Black men and women into the slave ship hold,
And we sailed away from the sun to the New World's cold.

Don't think we took it calmly, for we did not—
No! We left our own brand of forget-me-not!

The truth about the slave trade remains yet untold,
Of our warriors battling, brave and bold!

Of Black men who arrived across a wild sea
And pledged openly that they'd always be free!

JUNIOR: (*Steps into center stage with others.*) Brother and Sister Africans, there are five hundred of us here —five hundred that they would doom to a life of slavery. We are chained together here, ready to be sold on their auction block. But, I ask you—would you live as slaves or die, as free men???

ALL: Die, die, die!

JUNIOR: There is the mighty sea, beckoning to us. Across it lies Mother Africa. Let us walk into the sea, walking back across it toward Africa. And if we should drown, we do so as free men and women, enternally free! And the world will know that the people of Africa love freedom so much that they will destroy themselves for that freedom! Let us march!

ALL:
Let us march!
March!
March toward freedom!
What can the sea do to us?
Kill us?
We've died before!
We'll die again!
March, brother!
March, sister!
Mother!
Brother!
March!
March into the sea!

(*Music rises, loud, pulsating, then carries under as* MRS. BLACK *speaks.*)

MRS. BLACK: Only the ocean floor knows how many Black men and women lie in the graves beneath it. The silly songs of Stephen Foster become even sillier when we face the truth that slaves burned down plantations, put spiders in old master's soup, and sometimes killed him while he was asleep. Anyone who thinks that slavery represented the "good old days" ought to look at the record! Let the record be read and read well!

MISS BLACK:
Yes, they killed me and they raped me—
They sold my man far-off, away from me.
They put a badge of color, decried being Black—
They made it symbolic of the mighty slaver's track!
Their standard said whites could be swarthy and
 blond,
For this was the complexion of which whites were
 fond—

Their standard said: Chain Negroes to the slaver's track—
Never admitting you could be many colors, yet *black*!
Their standard reduced poor Black folks into a search for hair—
Their standard made some Black folks search for what they called "good hair"—

Their standard made many start to search for something else again,
Forgetting "Divide and Conquer" is an old, old refrain!
They sold my mother's body into a town called New Orleans—
They sold my father into Georgia with all his dreams!
White scoundrels raped my family in a manner yet unseen,
Yet cursed me because I was born "in-between".

(*Singing*)

I been 'buked and I been scorned—
I been talked about sure as you borned!

I been 'buked and I been scorned!
I been talked about sure as you born!
I been 'buked and I been scorned!
I been talked about sure as you born!
I ain't gon' lay religion down!
I been 'buked and I been scorned—
I been talked about sure as you born!

MRS. BLACK: (*As music carries under*)
While I was being 'buked and scorned, Truth was being torn from the history books—
One such truth was that I was in the New World before it was born.
Let the record be read and read well—
In 1626 when New York City was a Dutch outpost called New Amsterdam
Eleven African slaves were imported.

They lived on the fringe of what is now The Bowery.
These Africans built a wagon road to the upper part
   of the Settlement—
To a place the Dutch called Haarlem, spelled with
   two "a's".
Yes! Let the record be read and read well—
Eighteen years later these Africans were supported
   by rank-and-file white colonists
When they petitioned the Dutch for freedom.
They received it and they settled in a swampland
   which they built into a prosperous community.
That community is today known as Greenwich Village.
And all you Black children in the world out there—
When you think about Third Avenue,
Think about those eleven Africans!
When you see Greenwich Village,
Remember those eleven Africans!

Race relations in New Amsterdam?
They were relatively cordial.
Black men were artisans, craftsmen, executioners,
   doctors.
Many well-to-do Negroes owned slaves—
Black slaves and white slaves—
Among the prominent Black families were Domingo
   Antony, who owned land on Canal Street,
And Catalina Antony who owned land on what is now
   Pell Street,
And Annie d'Angelo, who owned the site of the
   original Madison Square Garden,
And Solomon Pieters who owned thirty acres of land
   at Twenty-third Street and Fifth Avenue
Where the Flatiron Building now stands.
And Black people owned much of the land that is
   now around
Astor Place, City Hall Park and the site of the Woolworth Building!

Let the record be read and read well—
For little color discrimination existed in seventeenth-century New York.

People of different races attended the same
  churches, drank in the same taverns.
Pieter Stuyvesant said everything was in God's bless-
  ing as a result of the employment of Negroes.
He said in 1660: "Let the free and the company's
  Negroes
Keep good watch on my Bowery!"
Discrimination in seventeenth-century New York
  was integrated.
It was a matter of caste and class. Then—
The British came. They seized New Amsterdam and
  named it New York.
They instituted chattel slavery and brought rigid
  slave codes.
Color discrimination became a reality,
And the Rights of Man were denied Black people.

JUNIOR: (*Singing*)
And I couldn't hear nobody pray,
Couldn't hear nobody pray.
Oh, 'way down yonder by myself,
And I couldn't hear nobody pray!

MRS. BLACK: (*As music carries under*) In 1682 an edict was passed stating Negroes could no longer be buried in Trinity Church cemetery. The land owned by Negroes was willed to the British Crown. The manumission of slaves became increasingly difficult.... The doctrine of non-violence was then non-existent. Black people struck back, helped by poor whites and Indians. One insurrection followed another. Fire was the Black people's chief weapon, and they nearly burned the city to the ground. It was during that period that the New York City Fire Department came into existence. But you don't read that in the history books or see that on television or movie screens....

(*Music: A defiant chord, then:*)

ACT ONE

MISS BLACK:
Tell Pharaoh
To let my story be told!
My story about Crispus Attucks,
The first man to fall in the American Revolution—
Pharaoh!
Let my story be told!
Let my story be told
About the Black women who fought the Revolution,
About the five thousand Black men who fought then
As Black Africa saved white America!
Tell Pharaoh
To talk about Peter Salem
And Salem Poor
And tavern-owner Sam Fraunces—
His daughter saved George Washington's life!

Let my story be told
Of the way I was 'buked and scorned,
The way I was talked about sure as you're born—
Let my story be told
Of white America turning on Black Africa
When Africa had saved it!

Let my story be told
Of the way America stereotyped me,
Villified me when it knew my deeds!
This was no accident!
This inglorious, infamous act was to destroy Black people,
To make proud people beggars in the American drama!

SENIOR:
Yes! Let my story be told—
Of the African Free School,
Of James Hewlett and the African Grove Theatre
Who performed classics in 1821.
Let my story be told
Of hoodlums wrecking it,
Of the great Ira Aldridge going abroad,

Playing before royalty because he couldn't play here!
Yes, Pharaoh!
Let my story be told
Of the way you ignored my heroism during the Civil
  War,
Of the way the slave walked off the plantation and
  joined the Union Army
And broke the Confederacy's economic back!
Let my story be told
Of the way I created minstrelsy,
Yet you stole it and used it against me!
Let my story be told
Of the way I paraded through our history
For we'd have no history without me,
Black me!

MISS BLACK: (*Singing*)
I am a poor pilgrim of sorrow,
I'm left in this wide world to roam,
No thoughts have I of tomorrow
Except to make Heaven my home.
Sometimes I am tossed and driven,
Sometimes I don't know where to roam,
But I heard of a city called Heaven,
I'm trying to make it my home!
My mother done reached that pure glory,
My father's still walking in sin—
My brothers and sisters won't own me
Because I'm trying to get in!
Sometimes I am tossed and driven,
Sometimes I don't know where to roam—
I've heard of a city called Heaven,
I'm trying to make it my home.

MRS. BLACK: (*As music carries under*)
Harlem lay dormant until the mid-nineteenth
  century....
Mid-nineteenth century Harlem was peopled by
  crude squatters who lived in cottages.
Industrial development, business expansion, im-
  proved transportation,

And the arrival of the so-called foreign-born transformed Harlem,
By 1886 three elevated lines reached the community. Fashionable New Yorkers fled from Lower Manhattan To build New York's first suburb: Harlem!

MISS BLACK: (*With spectacles, as a wealthy white dowager*) I remember Harlem. We built our house there in 1888 and, oh, it was swank, high-fashion, with carriages, mansions, and the very best people. We were careful to tell people we lived in Harlem, NOT New York City. The city was for foreigners! Why, in 1893 the *Harlem Monthly Magazine* wrote that Harlem was the future center of fashion, culture, and intelligence. But, in the early 1900s something happened: The news got out that they were opening a Lenox Avenue subway. By 1904 all of Harlem's vacant land had been sold. Wild speculation raged. And the bust followed the boom. Houses stood vacant, waiting to be rented. But the high rents scared off the general population and—this is what happened.

JUNIOR: (*To* SENIOR, *who plays a white realtor now.*) Mr. Man, my name is Philip. My friend, Soloman and I have been talking about Harlem. We figured that if Negroes moved in there, you could get twice and maybe three times the rent that white folks would pay.

SENIOR: (*The white realtor*) Rent to colored folks? In Harlem? Boy, you've got to be kidding.

JUNIOR: No, sir. Colored folks living downtown, getting beat up when they come home. Menfolks have to meet one another on corners and walk home together to keep from getting beat up. Gangs are going into colored homes, beating women and children. Colored folks would just love to have a place all their own so they wouldn't be bothering white folks. And they'll pay. That means money for you. And some for me.

SENIOR: Money? . . Well, now, boy, you all do love to sing and dance and pray and be off to yourselves, don't you? Now, I ain't thinking about money alone, but this is my chance to help you all out. So you rent these apartments to your folks, for that's a real Christian act—especially if you can rent to colored folks at three times what white folks would pay.

JUNIOR: Boss, you and me—we sure ain't going to die poor!

SENIOR: Dying poor ain't Christian.

JUNIOR: Sure ain't, boss! You know what I think was the meaning of Moses not making the Promised Land and Jesus dying like he did? It was to show folks how not to act!

SENIOR: Boy, we'll talk all that religion after you rent to colored folks for three times what white folks would pay!

MRS. BLACK: Rent to colored folks for three times what white folks would pay. It wasn't difficult, for this is what went on in too many homes—

MISS BLACK: (*Appears in center stage as a teenager*) Mama! Mama!

MRS. BLACK: (*Appears as her mother.*) What is it? (*Then*) Lord, my child been beat up again! Lemme look at you, girl.

MISS BLACK: Mama, I ain't hurt bad. Not as bad as one of them. I took off my shoe when them two boys come up to me and said something nasty. And I parted his hair with the heel of my shoe.

MRS. BLACK: (*Happily*) You did? (*Then*) But, child, the Lord says you got to turn the other cheek.

MISS BLACK: I turned the other cheek, Mama—after I hit the other one with my fist and bloodied his nose.

MRS. BLACK: You did? That's good! (*Then*) No! that's bad! ... Lord, I ain't never gonna get used to this North. I couldn't get used to down home, either. The

Bible says you is supposed to love your neighbor, but they beat us down there and up here they come in your house and beat on you! Lord, what we gonna do?

MISS BLACK: Mama, stop calling on the Lord, 'cause He can get all confused if these white folks calling on Him to get rid of us while you calling on Him to help us!

MRS. BLACK: Girl, you shut your mouth! We already got white folks down on us, so don't go getting the Lord down on us, too!

MISS BLACK: I don't mind the Lord being down on us, 'cause He ain't beating on us like white folks is.

MRS. BLACK: He ain't gonna get a chance to beat on you 'cause if you keep on blaspheming His name, I'm gonna work on your backside 'fore he reaches you. I sure wish your Pa had a lived.

MISS BLACK: They'd a beat on him, too! How many nights did he come in here and knock over a chair or bang the wall? I used to lay in my bed and hear you all arguing about any little thing and one night I heard you tell him: "Go fight where you got mad!" And he told you: "If I did, you'd be a widow before you could bat an eye!" (*Then*) Mama, I don't wanta stay here no more. I'm tired—tired of fighting to get in the front door, tired of walking the street and having men grab at me! This ain't what you and Papa walked all the way north for! If I don't do something about it, I ain't gonna be able to look you in the face or to even remember Papa for the man he really was!

MRS. BLACK: Yes, child! We going from here. A man come around the church the other day and he told us about apartments in Harlem, renting to colored folks. Six-room apartments for thirty-four dollars a month, with all modern conveniences except steam heat and bathrooms. Lots of colored folks talking about moving there. You think you'd like it?

MISS BLACK: Like it? Oh, Mama, please! Let's move. Move to where we can live like people and not be afraid. You can go out to your church groups, and I won't have to meet you after, and maybe boys can come down to see me one at a time and not have to bring their friends to keep from getting jumped on the way home. Mama, let's move. . . .

(*Music rises, then:*)

JUNIOR: (*Singing*)
On that great-getting-up morning,
Fare thee well, fare thee well!
On that great-getting-up morning
Fare thee well, fare thee well—
There's a better day-a-coming,
Fare-thee-well, fare-thee-well!

MRS. BLACK: (*As the music carries under*) And so the first Black families moved into Harlem. And the whites resisted. And the Black folks kept moving in and the whites kept fighting back.

To the land north of 110th Street came Southerners escaping from physical lynchings, West Indians escaping from escaping from economic lynchings, and northern Black folks escaping the terror they knew in Lower Manhattan. They met in the land north of 110th Street and they brought with them their folkways, their mores, their religiosity, and their dogged determination.

There was a subway stop at 135th Street and Lenox Avenue—a stop known as the Pearly Gates. It was also known as one of the stops on the Underground Railroad. Black people milled around that subway stop daily, waiting to meet newly arrived relatives from the South, The West Indies, or Lower Manhattan. There a drama as magnificent as the Exodus was played daily. A Southern Black laborer appeared and looked at the crowd of people. . . .

ACT ONE

SENIOR: (*In center stage*) Lord! I ain't never seen so many colored folks since you sent the Word! . . . Why, this ground here is hard—real hard, real concrete! Wonder how a body plants corn in these parts? . . . Look at them buildings. One, two, three, four stories high! They mighty high for chicken coops! . . . Ummmm. Kinda cold. The sun ain't warm like it is down home. Mary Belle and the young'uns ain't gonna like this a speck. . . . Everybody here wearing shoes, too! Must cost a heap of money to be staying up here. . . . I sure wish I was back home with Mary Belle and my children right now. . . . Well, I can't be back 'cause the land ain't fallow and ain't nothing growing, nothing. Schoolhouse is six miles away and the young'uns can't learn nothing. I got to rassle with this here concrete and tear it up so's something can grow for my wife and kids. Yeah, old concrete! You and me is gonna have one jim-dandy fight and I'm gonna win!

(*He returns to his lectern.*)

MISS BLACK: (*Appears as a teenager.*) Lenox Avenue and 135th Street! That's what the sign says. What're all these folks looking at? . . . Mama, I sure wish you coulda come with me. It's lonesome and I'm scared. Lord, I wish I had the fare! I'd take the next thing smoking right on outa this city! . . . But, what would I do if I did? Ain't no work down home for a colored girl 'cept cleaning up after white folks and having their men trying to flirt with you. I got to stay here where colored folks is free! . . . Mama, I'm scared—scared of this place and its people. It's big! And everybody's looking at me, but nobody sees me. . . . I'm gonna work real hard up here, Mama, then I'm coming back home to stay. You hear me, Mama? . . . Oh, who'm I lying to? I can't go home no more 'cause home ain't got nothing for me! (*She returns to her lectern.*)

JUNIOR: (*Appears as a West Indian youth.*) This is New York. A strange place. No palm trees swaying. And the sun is not friendly. My people do not look like they do on the island. There is no warmth here in the people nor in the climate. . . . If I were home now, I'd be on the island shore, casting my net and the sun would be kissing my face. But, who can earn a living casting a net and having his face kissed by the sun? What hope is there at home except for tomorrow when I must live today? . . . New York, you shall not defeat me as you have so many of my people. You shall not send me running back to the island to drown your memories in rum. I shall love you, big city, if you love me—and fight you if you mistreat me! (*He returns to his lectern.*)

MRS. BLACK: (*Appears as a mother with children.*) Come on now, children. We at 135th Street and Lenox Avenue. Ohhh! Look at the buildings!. You reckon folks live that high off the ground? . . . Joseph, Junior, you stop that! We ain't down home now. We in the big city! . . . Lord, I sure wish my man was here with me 'cause I'm scared. Joseph, Senior, why you got to be off working in Atlantic City when I needs for you to be in New York with me and our children? . . . I know. I know. You work where there is work. But, this town is so *big*. Ain't right for a woman to be alone in it, much less with children. . . . What am I gonna do here where I don't know a living soul? Who gonna help me tend the children when they gets sick? Who gonna be my friends now? . . . Lord, I wish I was back home! . . . But, I can't go back home! No, sir! These young'uns got to grow up not being scared to walk into town! They got to get some learning and be somebody when they grows up. They got to have what I ain't never had! And they gonna get it! They gonna get it, else I'm gonna go to my grave trying to see that they do! Yes, Lord, they gonna get it! That they do! Yes, Lord, they gonna get it! (*She returns to her lectern.*)

ACT ONE

MISS BLACK(*Singing*)
Tramping, tramping,
Trying to make heaven my home—
I'm tramping, tramping,
Trying to make heaven my home!

(*The music carries under as the lights pick out* MRS. BLACK *at her lectern.*)

MRS. BLACK: Harlem life was difficult, but it was *fun*! There were churches and lodges and clubs and there was friendship on every block. There were such institutions as the Schomburg Collection where Negro history and culture were housed. And there was the Old Dutch Bell on Mt. Morris Park Hill and the Jumel Mansion and the 135th Street Library and the Savoy Ballroom and the Renaissance Casino. And there were legitimate theatres—first the Crescent on 135th Street, then the Lincoln, the Lafayette, and the Alhambra where sometimes you could see vaudeville skits such as this—

JUNIOR: (*Meets* SENIOR *in center stage.*) Hey, man! I didn't know that was you!

SENIOR: I didn't know that was you, either! I sure am glad to see you. I just ran into—

JUNIOR: I saw him yesterday and he said—

SENIOR: That ain't what he told me. He told me—

JUNIOR: Oh, he told me that, too. But, he told that woman next door to him—

SENIOR: I didn't know that about her. I thought she was—

JUNIOR: I thought she, too, until the other day when her doctor told me—

SENIOR: He said *that* about her? Last week he told me—

JUNIOR: He told me that, too, but you know what I think? I think—

SENIOR: You've got to be kidding! I thought—

JUNIOR: I thought so too! I ain't never heard of a doctor's wife telling him not to charge another woman unless—

SENIOR: That's what I thought, too! But, she's a good girl. A real good girl! She goes to bed every night at 9 p.m.

JUNIOR AND SENIOR: (*In unison*) Then she gets up at three A.M. and goes home!

JUNIOR: You know something, man? The thing I like about running into you is—a man can always get into a *good* conversation!

(*They go off to their respective lecterns.*)

MRS. BLACK: One of the grave problems of being a Black American is that each generation must discover you. This is part and parcel of America's attempt to destroy Black people. It states, in effect, that it was all right to lynch, cheat, and kill the so-called Old Negro, and it justifies many a guilt complex. The reality is there has never been an "old Negroes."

Whites discovered the so-called New Negro in the nineteen-twenties and there flowered in Harlem what came to be known as the Black Renaissance. The arts flourished. Many thought this was a millenium. Columbia students ran around Harlem measuring Negroes' heads. Rich white folks invaded Harlem night spots and many found Negroes exotic.

The Depression of 1929 flooded the nation and drowned the Black Renaissance. Grown men, able-bodied, stood on 125th Street with apples for sale. They wore signs: "Unemployed. Please buy apples." America trembled. Unemployed workers searched garbage cans for food. Many milled together into communities of hungry, homeless men who squatted along riverfronts in crude cottages that became known as Hoovervilles. The nation cried, and Harlem cried with it, for both had the Blues and this is the way poet James C. Morris described them:

These are the Blues,
a longing beyond control
Left on an unwelcome doorstep,
slipping in when the door is opened.

These are the Blues:
a lonely woman crouched at a bar,
gulping a blaze of Scotch and rye,
using a tear for a chaser.

The Blues are fears that
blossom like ragweeds
in a well-kept bed of roses.

Nobody knows how tired I am,
And there ain't a soul who gives a damn!

(*A strong musical note, then she continues.*)

The election of Franklin Delano Roosevelt stopped America from searching for the Good Old Days. The nation began to dig its way out of the Depression and Harlem dug, too. The Federal Theatre, the Rose McClendon Players, and later the American Negro Theatre attempted to build Black theatres in Harlem and, in so doing, they launched many careers.

The child of Harlem had the will to live, to survive, to make it. He knew his Black identity and in the nineteen thirties he made up his own language which he threw into the faces of whites much as they resorted to Yiddish, Italian, or Spanish.

JUNIOR: (*Meets* SENIOR *in center stage.*) Man! What you putting down?

SENIOR: I'm putting down all skunks, punks and a hard hustle!

JUNIOR: Dad, I ain't dead, but I'm looking for some bread. I am like the bear. I ain't nowhere. I'm like the bear's brother. I ain't gonna get no further. In other words, I'm like the black night facing the white day. I am up tight and I don't want to stay that way!

SENIOR: You beating a dead horse to death 'cause I ain't no man of great wealth. If I'm lying, I'm flying. In fact, Jack, if I'm lying, God's gone to Jackson, Mississipi and you know he wouldn't be hanging around in *that* place!

JUNIOR: You done come up crummy when I need you, Sonny. You have been a social hanger when I need a banger. You have low-rated me, ill-fated me, disgraced me and abraced me. I thought you was my main man and you have showed your can. You have been a drag and darn near a hag. You have brought me down, clown. You are supposed to be hip as a whip, but you are a crumb, chum, and if I could afford a broom, I would sweep you off the scene, Gene!

SENIOR: You may be a poet and not know it. Go on, Gates, and solid swing, but I am forced to tell you just one thing: Your eyes may flash fire and you may spit, but none of my green bread will you git!

(*They walk away from each other.*)

MRS. BLACK: Translation? One Harlemite was trying to borrow money from another, was rejected, hence the retort.... There were other things in Harlem. We partied. We dug Joe Louis. And we dug the Yankees before the team's owners got pompous. And we Strolled....

JUNIOR: Seventh Avenue was once a fashionable, tree-lined boulevard, sometimes called Colored Folks' Broadway. City authorities fined building superintendents for allowing rubbish to accumulate. People glared you out of existence if you were seen improperly dressed or misbehaving there. And you got tongue-lashed at home for shaming the family and the neighborhood. Besides, Black policemen like Brisbane, Brown, Penderghast, and Lacey kept

Seventh Avenue orderly. They would go up side your head in a minute, then—since they knew all families around—they'd tell your Dad and he'd go up side the rest of your anatomy.

Seventh Avenue was where you strolled those exciting Sunday afternoons. No one who knew Harlem from the 1920s through the 1940s can forget Strolling.

We youngsters had suits issued by the WPA. That's the Works Progress Administration, or—for you young bloods—the granddaddy of this here Antipoverty Program. We had tailors "drape" these suits, then we put on our shirts, ties, and hats and called on our young ladies.

Strolling was seemingly casual, but it was exciting, with a point and a purpose. You had to walk with your right leg dipping a bit, resembling a limp. You and your young lady started just below 116th Street, moving north on the west side of the avenue. In front of the Regent Theatre you met a couple. The male tipped his hat to your young lady and you responded, smartly, in an almost military manner. Invariably, the couple invited you to a "function" or a party. You told them: "Lay the pad number on us and we'll pick up that action later. You dug your Stroll. We got to dig ours."

On you moved, meeting and greeting folks. You reached 125th Street one hour and a half later. At the Theresa you saw Bill Robinson, George Whitshire, Adam Clayton Powell, Jr., Paul Robeson, Ralph Cooper, Pigmeat Markham, Canada Lee, Dick Campbell or Joe Louis, waving at you, acting like they knew you even if they didn't. They had less ego than many of our present-day celebrities.

Scores of other Strollers brought news from all parts of Harlem to 125th Street. Then—replenished and recognized—you Strolled north again, knowing you had the "sharpest Chick" in the world and that you were the "Sharpest Cat" that ever Strolled!

Three hours after the start of your Stroll, you "fell" into Henry's Sugar Bowl at 134th Street and Seventh Avenue. You had a malted, met other friends, then started downtown again. You told the world: "This is Black Me in my Harlem. I belong here and I'm somebody!"

Man, we Strolled!

Strolling is gone from Harlem, possibly never to return. The Establishment's standards claw at our culture, malign our community and its beautiful people. Somehow, some way, as we moved toward the mainstream, I wish we could Stroll with our true Black Identities, telling the world: "This is Beautiful Me in my Beautiful Black Harlem. Dig me! If you really dig, you can reap a great harvest!"

MISS BLACK: (*As* JUNIOR *returns to lectern*) While we were Strolling a second Dred Scott decision was being written in New York City—a decision that was to enslave Harlem, Bedford-Stuyvesant, South Jamaica, and the South Bronx. The slaveholders now sat in big offices behind fat cigars, directing bank operations. In the nineteen-thirties these banks foreclosed on loans and mortgages in Harlem. They noted the high rents being paid there and they established the Savings Trust Company. Reporter Ted Poston states that in the very next year they formed the Mortgage Conference of New York. They confined Black and Spanish-speaking people to definite areas. They induced realtors to refuse minority groups space in certain areas. They denied mortgage financing for maintaining homes in habitable conditions. They made successful operations at reasonable rent levels impossible. The United States Justice Department proved all of this in 1946. The Court issued a decree forbidding such practices. But, the Court could not prevent banks from doing *individually* what they were forbidden to do *collectively*.

MRS. BLACK: This action, written in infamy, boxed in the Black American's community and allowed it to deteriorate because his misery made others rich! Physical lynchings were no longer needed. Profits could be made by maiming families through poverty, disease, disillusionment, and death. This conspiracy could destroy family structures in ways never dreamed of by exconvicts and rogues. This conspiracy chased those aggressive, stubborn Harlem children from the land of their birth while the white hoodlum reaped untold wealth from drugs, defective buildings, graft, and human misery. With the stubborn Harlem children out of the community, there was no need to spend money for essential services, to meet legitimate human demands, or to recognize the people of Harlem as human beings! The battle of the Harlem child had, in the last analysis, been won by the hoodlum! That hoodlum had placed every allegedly anti-social act committed by oppressed Black people squarely on the table where Black leadership would have to cringe and apologize for its existence!

The rape of the Black American was complete!

MISS BLACK: (*Singing*)

I'm so glad trouble don't last always—
I'm so glad trouble don't last always—
Oh, my Lord,
Oh, my Lord!
What shall I do?

MRS. BLACK: (*As music carries under*)

Frustration raged.
Hungry, homeless families walked cold city streets.
Job discrimination was a fact of life on 125th Street
And everywhere and insults filled your ears in local stores.
Stories of lynchings and physical abuse came out of the South:
The Scottsboro Boys and Angelo Herndon were targets of abuse,

And wrath and vengeance consumed the hearts and minds of Harlem's people.
The voices of A. Philip Randolph and Adam Clayton Powell, Jr. shouted for freedom and justice
And then—
Rioting erupted on 125th Street.

(*Music rises, then carries under.*)

The strength of power lies in its manipulation. While the world battled poverty, its power structures conspired. There arose in Germany conspirators financed by people outside and inside that nation.

Stories seeped out about Jews being burned in gas chambers. No one cared to believe it because the Nazi army had been built to destroy Communism, not us.... The world went up in flames in 1939 and once again it became a battle for democracy. People in Harlem wondered how America could fight for democracy abroad when it didn't exist at home.

Something called Selective Service came into existence—and this was after all America had piously shouted about "No More War!"—shouted this while fascist Italy raped Ethiopia and Franco destroyed the Spanish Republic... Yet the draft became a reality. And the Cats everywhere worried. You could hear them up and down the streets of Harlem....

JUNIOR: (*As he meets* SENIOR *in center stage.*) Man, this draft is giving me a cold!

SENIOR: You? For years I been trying to get a government job and now I'm liable to get exactly the one I do not want!

JUNIOR: I hope that after this action, I don't face no *inaction*.

SENIOR: Things is bad! I hear that Cats are jumping off closets, barefooted, trying to get flat feet so they can beat this jive! Me—I am going to be 4F from heart failure, which I get every time I go to my mailbox.

ACT ONE

JUNIOR: Man, don't you sing the Blues to me when I got'em. You married and supporting a family!

SENIOR: Let me take you to school, fool! I been trying to get that wife of mine to go to work for years. Soon as I fall down to the draft board and get a deferment 'cause I'm supporting her, that woman goes out and gets a job. I told her: "You better get on down there and quit that job fast—like yesterday!" I said: "Baby, I'm working on keeping this deferment!"

JUNIOR: Deferment? Man, they have taken that word out of the dictionary. I know a Cat who has no arms. They drafted him into the Army and he asked the Man: "What am I going to do here with no arms?" The Man told him: "You see that fellow over there drawing a pail of water? Well, he's blind. You tell him where to put the water!"

(They walk off, shaking their heads.)

MRS. BLACK: Despite all the objections and protestations, Black men did what they have done since the founding of this nation. They went off and fought the war.

Suddenly, it became possible to walk from 116th Street to 125th Street in less than an hour and a half. For the young men were all away, and the people you met had their hearts and minds with those who were away.... And the streets lay crying, lay crying alone, for their youth had been taken from them. Some were to die on alien soil. Others were to return and move to suburbia. The streets probably knew this before anyone else, and so they lay crying, lay crying alone, for their children—their children had been taken from them.

MISS BLACK: *(Singing)*
Sometimes I feel like a motherless child,
Sometimes I feel like a motherless child,

Sometimes I feel like a motherless child,
A long ways from home,
A long ways from home!

(*The lights have begun to dim as the entire* COMPANY *sings with her as the curtain falls.*)

Curtain

End of Act One

Act Two

(*The lights fade in around the* Company. Miss Black *is in center stage, singing.*)

Miss Black: (*Singing*)
Sometimes I feel like a motherless child,
Sometimes I feel like a motherless child,
Sometimes I feel like a motherless child,
A long ways from home,
A long ways from home!

Mrs. Black: (*As music carries under*)
Freedom is anything but free.
Its cost is human lives and sacrifices,
And time, unpaid for time.
Freedom's cost is a mother's tears,
An agonizing shriek in the night for a son
Digging a foxhole on foreign soil
As bullets spit death!

Miss Black: (*As a war mother*) Telegram from the War Department. My son died a hero's death. They gonna send me a big check for his insurance. Money I ain't never seen before. Gonna be able to stack all that cash up in a row bigger'n me. Gonna have a big medal, too, pinned on me by the government. Gonna take a day off from scrubbing floors and go on down to Washington and get myself all honored. Yes, indeed! Gonna take that medal and put it right beside my husband's medal! I got no husband now. I got no son. I got nothing but heartaches and medals!

Mrs. Black: (*As a war wife*) Telegram from the War Department. My husband died a hero's death. I'm going to Washington, D.C. and get myself a medal and I'll get his insurance. I'll have my pictures in the papers and people will sing our praises. But, when my child cries out for his father, what will I say?

Whose hand will I reach for in the lonely hours of the night? . . . I swear to God that government ought to be run by mothers! They'd never send sons and husbands out to fight and die!

SENIOR: Telegram from the War Department. My son is dead. Lord, it seems like I'm dead, too. I done mopped floors and washed dishes and lifted concrete and shoveled coal and lugged ice and cleaned slime from spitoons so that boy could grow up and get some learning. I recollect when he graduated, he said to me, says: "Dad, you gonna retire now. I'm gonna take good care of you." Well, he took care of me all right—out there fighting for something he ain't got at home. Out there dying so folks can kill his brothers!

MISS BLACK: (*Singing*)
Nobody knows the trouble I see—
Nobody knows my sorrows—
Nobody knows the troubles I see
Glory, Hallejuah!
Sometimes I'm up, sometimes I'm down,
Oh, yes, Lord!
Sometimes I'm almost to the ground!
Oh, yes, Lord!
Nobody knows the trouble I see—
Nobody knows my sorrow—
Nobody knows the trouble I see—
Glory, Hallejuah!

MRS. BLACK: (*As music carries under*)
Peace came to the world in 1945. But—
Peace is an interlude between wars,
A time-out, and intermission for the mighty to regroup their forces
And prepare to cut down another generation.
Peace is a nightmare to the mighty,
A threat to its power and position.
The Cold War replaced the hot war during this intermission,

And the world's powers raved and ranted at each other,
And hysteria reigned!
The fearful fifties saw America in flight,
From self, into self.
Hysterical lies wrecked careers and human lives
And we laid to waste the Bill of Rights
To prove we were not Reds.
McCarthyism struck terror into the hearts and minds of people everywhere—

(JUNIOR *and* SENIOR *meet in center stage.* JUNIOR *is wary as they meet.*)

SENIOR: Hey, there, Brother! Don't you know me?

JUNIOR: Man, I got to be careful! This Man is coming down hard. They giving a loyalty oath on my job!

SENIOR: Yeah? I hear of a Cat uptown who got fired because he went to a Paul Robeson concert! You know all them Cats we used to know who had red hair that we called Red!? Well, those Cats have dyed their hair! (*He laughs.*)

JUNIOR: It ain't funny! Do you know the Man came to my house because he wanted me to sign a loyalty oath so I could keep my job emptying bed pans in a government hospital??? I thought he was joking, but he kept on talking about loyalty and disloyalty. So I gave him a bunch of names of congressmen that I thought were disloyal to this nation. I even gave him the name and address of the Head Man of the Ku Klux Klan! He was not impressed! Then, the Man asked me if I wanted to keep my job and I was *pressed!*

SENIOR: If you need any help, I can add to your list: The White Citizens Council, some drug connections and pushers, and some. . . .

JUNIOR: (*Interrupts*) Man, I do *not* need your list! In fact, the Man has his own list of some of my friends who have given parties and invited white folks to their homes—including you.

SENIOR: Hell, white folks have been coming to my house for years, collecting rent, or insurance, or selling me beat-up goods. It is about time some of them came to my house as *friends*!

JUNIOR: It is the *wrong* time! Nowadays if you have white friends, it means they might be suspected of being Red, which means you are guilty of association with folks who are a threat to this nation! In other words, Daddy-O, if you are a good white, you ain't right, 'cause that means you're Red and you and your friends are dead! And if you are Black, you had better stay 'way back 'cause you and your train can get run off the track!

SENIOR: Brother, your poetry is fine and it is mellow, but I'm gonna hip you up to my kind of fellow. I done fought every war this nation has seen and I don't intend to get caught in-between! I'm gonna get what's due me no matter what folks say, and anybody who don't like it can meet me down the way! I helped build this nation from bottom to top, and there ain't nobody gonna get me to leave or stop! Furthermore, I ain't out to do nobody in as long as he respects me and my kin! I do not hate white, red, Black, green, or in-between, but if I get pushed, I get mighty mean! The Devil is the Devil in many ways, but I ain't letting him mess with me the rest of my days!

JUNIOR: Right on, Brother! You fight on! but, you let me be while you holler so I can make a solid dollar! So—you do me a favor. Just stay away from me for about ten years—if this jive is over by then. If it ain't—well, man, I'll tell you when!

(*He gets on back to his lectern.* SENIOR *returns to his.*)

MRS. BLACK:
Yes!
McCarthyism struck terror into the hearts and
    minds of people everywhere
As bestiality displaced humanity,

And dissent was silenced—
A silence that made Korea a reality
That we buried yesterday, yet festers today
And becomes a running sore throughout our history!
America sought suburbia in the nineteen-fifties,
Leaving the cities for the impoverished and downtrodden,
The displaced and the disadvantaged.
A new stereostype spread its wings and did to Harlem
What black-faced comics had done to Black people long ago,
And Black communities became places from which one had to flee
As though one had the plague!
But stubborn is the child of the African mother,
The most avid seeker of the American Dream,
Reaching, reaching,
Believing always in tomorrow
And the Black Revolution thrust itself upon the scene,
A Revolution as old as the nation.
In a small parish in Clarendon County, South Carolina
The Reverend J.A. DeLaine exhorted his followers:

SENIOR: Oh, the Voice of God has roared in my ears this terrible day, charging us with the duty of saving white children that they may grow up to be our brothers, of saving the lives of all those who have been taught hate instead of love. In the words of St. Paul: "When I was a child, I spake as a child, I thought as a child, I understood as a child, but when I became a man, I put away childish things. And now abideth Faith, Hope and Love, and the greatest of these is Love!"

MISS BLACK: Yes! Love!

SENIOR: Oh, yes! The Voice of God has roared in my ears, testing my faith—by letting them kill my beloved children—testing me as Job was tested, as the Children of Israel were tested—as our people have been tested through nearly 300 years of slavery! Testing to see if God's work can be done on Earth as it is in heaven! And, oh, my friends, it will be done!

MISS BLACK: God's work will be done!

SENIOR: For even when the Law had been read and the signs that read: "This is for white" and "This is for Black" have been burned, still shall there be lynch mobs, still shall there be deaths! There will be more testing, more suffering!

MISS BLACK: Preach to 'em!

SENIOR: But, let not your heart be troubled, for the Seventh Seal shall be opened and they cannot hide!

MRS. BLACK: Ain't no hiding place down here!

SENIOR: And we cannot hide! We cannot hide by trying to kill the killers! For us to be worthy of our Great Duty us for us to teach them. Love on Earth—Soul! And how's that done?... Through Love! Yes, through Love! And where's that taught? In the home, in the Church, and in the Schools.... And that's the real meaning there, for there's no such thing as being separate but equal. The only thing a man learns when he's separate is that he's *not* equal!... Oh, they've beat on us and called us ugly apes, and men in high places have tried to double-talk us and sell us down the river in the name of Expediency! But, this I know! No nation in history has truly lived when it has sold a people down the river! Kill any section of a people and you kill a nation!

MISS BLACK: Yes, Lord!

MRS. BLACK: Yes, indeedy!

JUNIOR: Preach on, Brother!

SENIOR: Old Pharaoh killed the Children of Israel and God sent Moses down to let His people go! Greece had its slaves, and Greece fell! ... A large percentage of pagan Rome was Jewish, but when the Church took over, the Jews were expelled—and Rome fell! The Spanish had their Inquisition and Spain fell! Czarist Russia had it pogroms and Russia fell! Nazi Germany had its Jews and Gypsies, and Nazi Germany fell! The English had their Irish, their Africans, and Asians, and their islands of the sea—and England fell! America has had its Black people, its Latin people and its red people, and America has fallen! And the only way America can rise again is through you, my dark Brothers and Sisters! Will you give it a chance?

JUNIOR: Will it give me a chance?

SENIOR: It will have to because America likes to see others die, not Americans! And it's got to let us live for it to live! In my Father's House are many mansions. If it were not so, I would not have told you so.... And that means there's room for all—not up yonder in the sky, but here on Earth—for black, yellow, brown, red, white or any other color. And I'm going to see to that! I'm going to see to that or go rotting to my grave!

THE GROUP:
Yes, Lord!
Amen!
Amen! Amen!

ALL: (*Singing*)
Keep your hand on the plow, hold on!
Keep your hand on the plow, hold on!

MRS. BLACK: (*As music carries under*) To the highest court in the land Dr. DeLaine went with five other cases, and on May 17, 1954 the Supreme Court said:

JUNIOR: In *Sweat* versus *Painter*, supra., in finding that a segregated law School for Negroes could not provide them with equal educational opportunities, this Court relied in large part on those qualities which are incapable of objective measurement, but which make for greatness in a law school. In McLaurin versus Oklahoma State Regents, supra., the Court, in requiring that a Negro admitted to a white graduate school be treated like all other students again resorted to tangible considerations. ... "His ability to study, to engage in discussions, and exchange views with other students, and, in general, to learn his profession. Such considerations apply with added force to children in grade school. To separate them from others of similar age and qualifications solely because of their race generates a feeling of inferiority as to their status in the community that may affect their hearts and minds in a way unlikely to ever be undone."

Mrs. Black: The law was read, but not obeyed,
And vicious forces sought to evade it,
To drive deep despair into the hearts and minds of little children.
Reigns of terror were unleashed,
Striving to push back into the soil the seeds of truth
That refused to remain hidden there!

Flaming seeds scorched the soil of Alabama
And Little Rock, Arkansas—
And Florida,
And Louisiana,
And North Carolina,
And South Carolina,
And smeared the cities of Philadelphia and Baltimore
And Cambridge and Louisville and Atlanta
And Clinton and Albany
And blazed into the Mississippi night!

The Truth thrust its way upwards out of the soil,
Defying the cruel planter's hand, reaching towards
The rays of the sun!
The hearts and minds of little children erupted!
They erupted, breaking through concrete and stone.
They erupted, overflowing city streets,

Defying mad dogs and mad men who once struck terror
Into the hearts and minds of children.

Southern cities, northern cities,
Small towns and large towns and villages and hamlets
Shut their ears to the cry: "We shall overcome!"

Latrine legalism, moderation, gentility, and patience
And long lines of crooked thought sought to delay
The march towards the sunlight.

What price the right to protest,
Guaranteed nearly two hundred years ago?
Vicious dogs, firehoses, cruel epithets
To claw at the hearts and minds of little children. . . .

The world looked on, awe-stricken,
In wild disbelief, yet this was no new page
In the nation's history! No!
This was the result of three centuries' attempt to destroy
The hearts and minds of people!

But, volcanic truth
Soared inexorable from the soil,
Hurling challenges to those who had planted,
Shouting for new hands
To plow, to cultivate—
It challenged them in a way they have never before known,
Challenged them before a world assembly dominated by adults
Whose minds the planters had tried to twist years ago!

Twist some they did,
Black and brown and white
Into vineyards of impoverishment
Where Hope is an unknown word
And Yesterday dark despair and tomorrow is
A fleeting, still-born moment.

And Skid Row?
This is not Birmingham, Alabama nor Montgomery,

Nor Atlanta, nor any southern town—
This is New York
And Philadelphia
And Chicago—
Skid Rows where Black men and white men
Scrounge side by side in the gutter,
Playing out their last hopes together,
Playing them out because they could not train
  together!
This, too, is challenged—
This shall not last,
Nor shall resistance to the Law!

Innocent, indeed, are the hearts and minds of children,
But searching, too,
expressive,
Demanding when denied
Presenting new challenges that must be met,
Or chaos faced!

MISS BLACK AND COMPANY: (*Singing*)
Ohhh, Freedom! Ohhh, Freedom!
Oh, Freedom over me!
And before I'll be a slave,
I'll be buried in my grave
And go home to my Lord and be free!

MRS. BLACK: (*As music carries under*) The nineteen-fifties brought something else. In Montgomery, Alabama a woman named Rosa Parks got on a jimcrow bus and sat down up front. The driver ordered her:

JUNIOR: Move to the rear!

MISS BLACK: I moved yesterday. I'm too tired to move today!

MRS. BLACK: We're all tired!

MISS BLACK: Yes, tired. Tired of the aggravation and irritation!

MRS. BLACK: Tired of frustration and worriation!

MISS BLACK: Tired of being misused and abused.

MRS. BLACK: Tired of being used and confused!

TOGETHER: Tired! Tired! Tired!

JUNIOR: And all Montgomery walked. In the classic words of Martin Luther King, Jr., "We substituted tired feet for tired souls!"

MRS. BLACK:
Freedom's fires burned throughout the South,
And the blaze spread northward,
Searing the urban centers.
The voice of Malcolm X roared from Harlem,
And Black voices everywhere shouted at Pharaoh,
Telling him to let my people go now!
Insidious Pharaoh, venomous hate-spreader,
Created the backlash which is really a frontlash,
Created it and made Black people beggars in the American Dream,
Insisting upon God-given rights, yet being told:
"Be good, you Negroes, or we won't give you
What we have no right to keep from you in the first place!"
God, said Pharaoh, is white
And white is right!
But, stubborn is the child of the African mother,
Challenging, continuing to fight!
Cries of freedom rang out from everywhere!"

ALL: (*Singing*)
Good news! The chariot's coming!
Good news! The chariot's coming!
Good news! The chariot's coming!
I don't want to leave you behind!

MRS. BLACK: (*As music carries under*)
The nineteen-sixties were the destroying years,
The death-years, the violent years, the murderous years.
Assassination aborted the lives of
Patrice Lumumba, Medgar Evers, the four children of Birmingham,

John Fitzgerald Kennedy, Malcolm X, Lemuel Penn,
Viola Liuzzo, three youths in Mississippi
And Martin Luther King and Robert Francis Kennedy,
Plunging them into the earth in a downpour of discontent.
The pollution of our souls spread to the sea and sky,
And God cried for humanity!
Yes, God cried for humanity!

MISS BLACK AND COMPANY: (*Singing*)
All along my lonesome journey,
I want Jesus to walk with me.
All along my lonesome journey,
I want Jesus to walk with me!

Walk with me, Jesus,
Walks with me!
Walk with me, Jesus,
Walk with me!
All along my lonesome journey,
I want Jesus to walk with me!

MRS. BLACK: (*As song concludes*) Pharaoh did a little walking, too. And he wore hard-heeled shoes with taps on them. For things like this happened:

(JUNIOR *steps downstage with a suitcase that he is furiously closing.* SENIOR *appears.*)

SENIOR: Man, what are you doing? Going on vacation?

JUNIOR: No. I am leaving this metropolitan area once and for all. I'm glad you came over so I won't have to stop off at your house and say goodbye.

SENIOR: Leaving for good? I thought you said that only death could get you out of Greater New York!

JUNIOR: If there is one thing I dislike, it is Negroes who always have to go into ancient History! If you must know, the Shadow of Death is making me move! I have my car all gassed up and its nose is pointing towards Canada! So—goodbye.

Act Two

SENIOR: Wait! I heard the crime rate is going down and—there'll be less stealing by and by.

JUNIOR: I am not worried about stealing. That's as American as apple pie. In fact, white folks invented stealing. They stole the land from the red people and Black people from Africa! ... What I am running from is the political scene. At a party last night some folks got to talking about New York City having a Black mayor in the near future. And they looked straight at *me*!

SENIOR: You should be flattered!

JUNIOR: Flattered?? Man, I am shattered! The hypocrisy would make me cut my throat. The big shots from Washington on down have been on the public payroll for light years—and they have the nerve to talk about welfare! Five-dollar crooks do five years in the joint and five million-dollar crooks go away for six months—or less! And I ain't seen no soldiers go after southern lynch mobs! On the other hand, I am scared silly these dudes may invade South Africa—on the wrong side! ... Brother, I am battered and shattered over the thought of being a public official!

MISS BLACK: Honey! Honey, the motor's running!

SENIOR: Wait! You can't run out now when we're getting some kind of power.

JUNIOR: Power when you are broke is not power. It is rhetoric, which neither pays your rent, buys you food, or saves your life.

SENIOR: Go on and run! Thank God some of us can stay and face this!

JUNIOR: Yeah? Well, I forgot to tell you they also spoke of the day when there might be a Black president since nobody else seems to want the job. And they talked about your fine civic record!

SENIOR: They did????? (*He becomes wary.*)

MISS BLACK: Honey, let's go!

SENIOR: (*Reflecting*) Me? For President??? (*Suddenly*) Hey, wait a minute! You folks got any extra room in that car??

(*They go off together, returning to their respective lecterns.*)

MRS. BLACK:
Yes, sly Pharaoh! Sly, indeed!
But, stubborn is the child of the African mother,
And onward he went, claiming his birthright,
His heritage, which Pharaoh had denied him.
And Pharaoh knew that in denying him his heritage
The child of the African mother would seek just that
And become involved in sematics about whether he
    is Black
Or Afro-American or Negro, or truly integrated.
While Pharaoh had his foot upon his neck,
Stealing gold from South Africa,
And all the wealth of Asia and Africa,
Knowing always how to deal with latrine legalism
By uttering pious phrases—
And Pharaoh knew, too, that he was a genius at creat-
    ing family fights,
And he could get the American child of Africa to
    fight over petty things
While he stole from him the right to Harlem bought
    long ago
From the blood spilled in its streets!
Patient, indeed, are Pharaoh and his followers,
Ready to wait one hundred years to reassert his
    mastery,
Ready to offer New Deals and Fair Deals and New
    Frontiers and Great Societies,
Waiting, waiting for the day when he can send the
    bulldozers
Into the Harlem he did not mean to lose at the be-
    ginning of the twentieth century,

ACT TWO

Seeing the land for what it really is,
A choice location, a seat of Black power that must be integrated
To keep Black people subjected to the whims of their enemies!
Yet, Pharaoh, sly snake that he is,
Kept Black people suddenly learning things about themselves
And reveling in their newfound knowledge.
They learned that fifteen per cent of America's cowboys had been Black,
And they reveled in these stories untold by movies or television,
They told the story of Black Sam as though it had major significance
And all America loved it at a time when it had outlived what it meant to say:

JUNIOR: (*In center stage*) Somehow or other folks are just catching up to the fact that there was a Negro cowboy. If they'd bother to look they'd know that fifteen percent of America's cowboys were Black men. The baddest cowboy in the Old West was Black Sam. He was so bad that Webster had to look at him twice before he put the word "bad" in the dictionary.

Well, this western town was quiet one Sunday morning. You could smell the coffee brewing and the bacon frying, and from every house you could hear the chatter of folks as they put on their Sunday-go-to-meeting clothes for church. Suddenly-on top of the hill outside town there rode up this big Black cowboy. He was riding a bear. He rode that bear right on into town and stirred up so much dust that the town got quiet, the coffee stopped brewing, the bacon stopped frying, and houses got quiet because everybody and his brother got out of that town. It was so deserted that tumbleweeds flew up and down that town's street, crying about being so lonely.

This Black cowboy rode that bear right up in front of the town saloon. He told the bear to "Whoa!" and he got off it, wrapped his big hands around the bear's neck, choked it, then flung it across the street. Then he started into the saloon. He was so big he couldn't get into the door. He was seven feet tall and he weighed 475 pounds. He walked right on through the door, pulling off half the wall and half the ceiling. He brushed the dust from his shirt and walked up to the bar. The bartender and the sheriff were the only two people who hadn't run out of town. Both stood, trembling, 'cause they knew this was Black Sam, the baddest cowboy in the Old West. The Black cowboy ordered a bottle of red-eye and he broke the top of the bottle and poured down the liquor. He ordered another and he broke the top of that bottle, too, and he poured the liquor down again. He wiped his mouth and the sheriff trembled and decided he'd better get on the good side of Black Sam. He looked up at the Black cowboy and said:

"What about another bottle of red-eye on me?"

The Black cowboy shook his head and wiped some more liquor from his mouth and said:

"No, thanks. I got to get out of town before Black Sam gets here!"

MRS. BLACK: (*As* JUNIOR *returns to lectern.*)
All of this Pharaoh has denied us,
And we search for it and our identity
While he seeks untold wealth in undreamed of forms,
While we seek yet the story of Long Island, Brooklyn,
   the Bronx, Westchester, Soul City,
And the heroic souls who built these communities.
We seek yet to plant our feet on this earth,
To discover it, when this earth no longer has a meaning
For Pharaoh is reaching for the stars!

MISS BLACK: (*Crying out*)
Pharaoh!
Who is he?

MRS. BLACK:
The oppressor of Black people, brown people, red
  people, and yes, white people!
Pharaoh, let my people go!

MISS BLACK:
She's telling you, Pharaoh,
And I'm telling you, Pharaoh,
You'd better let us go!
Yes, old Pharaoh,
Let Black Africa go!
Let the islands of the sea go!

JUNIOR:
Pharaoh!
Let the children of Israel go!
Let there be brotherhood among the Arabs and Jews,
And let peace reign in Asia and everywhere!

MRS. BLACK:
We're telling you, Pharaoh—
Free the Latins,
The Indians here and those over there!
Pharaoh, Pharaoh! Let all people go!

SENIOR: Let all people go!
Let there be peace on this earth,
And freedom to build a tomorrow of brotherhood
Where we can plant the crops of goodness
And reap its harvest.
And God can then look down from His heaven
And smile because the brethern dwell together!

MRS. BLACK: Yes! Let all people go! When? When?

ALL: Now! Now! Now!

(*Music rises. The* COMPANY *sings:*)

COMPANY:
Go down, Moses
Way down in Egypt land,

Tell Old Pharaoh
To let my people go!
Tell Old Pharaoh
To let my people go!

(*This rises to a crescendo and the lights fade out.*)

Curtain

The End

www.ingramcontent.com/pod-product-compliance
Lightning Source LLC
Chambersburg PA
CBHW072014060426
42446CB00043B/2542